# Friends, Cliques, and Peer Pressure

## Be True to Yourself

Christine Wickert Koubek

**Enslow Publishers, Inc.**

40 Industrial Road          PO Box 38
Box 398                Aldershot
Berkeley Heights, NJ 07922   Hants GU12 6BP
USA                            UK

http://www.enslow.com

# Acknowledgments

*To my mother, Gail Wickert, my very first friend.*

*Thanks to my husband Tim, Gregg Weinlein, Jennifer Roy, Gabrielle Armenia, and Judi Murtha for all of their advice and support. And a very special thanks to the teens who shared their personal stories.*

**Library of Congress Cataloging-in-Publication Data**

Koubek, Christine Wickert.
　　Friends, cliques, and peer pressure : be true to yourself / Christine Wickert Koubek.
　　　　p. cm. — (Teen issues)
　　Includes bibliographical references and index.
　　ISBN 0-7660-1669-2 (hard)
　　1. Friendship in adolescence—Juvenile literature. 2. Interpersonal relations in adolescence—Juvenile literature. 3. Self-esteem in adolescence—Juvenile literature. 4. Cliques (Sociology)—Juvenile literature. [1. Interpersonal relations. 2. Friendship. 3. Peer pressure. 4. Cliques (Sociology)] I. Title. II. Series.
　　　　BF724.3.F64 K68　2001
　　　　158.2'5'0835—dc21

　　　　　　　　　　　　　　　　　2001006257

Printed in the United States of America

10 9 8 7 6 5 4 3 2

**To Our Readers:**
We have done our best to make sure all Internet Addresses in this book were active and appropriate when we went to press. However, the author and the publisher have no control over and assume no liability for the material available on those Internet sites or on other Web sites they may link to. Any comments or suggestions can be sent by e-mail to comments@enslow.com or to the address on the back cover.

**Illustration Credits:** Corel Corporation, p. 50; Diamar Interactive Corporation, pp. 6, 18, 53; Eyewire pp. 8, 16, 35, 40, 43; Skjold Photos, pp. 21, 27.

**Cover Photo:** Skjold Photos.

# Contents

# 1

# What Is a Friend?

*A year and a half ago two of my grandparents died. When I came back to school, my friends had decorated my locker and put lots of little gifts and cards inside it to make me feel better. My other grandparent died a couple of days before one of my best friend's birthday, so I missed her party. Everyone at the party made me cards and a tape of songs and them talking to make me feel better. It made me feel so good because they were all so supportive.*

Katie, age fifteen[1]

*I met all new friends when I got to high school and joined the choir. My friends now are more down-to-earth We're all in the cast together (Fiddler on the Roof), we relate to the same style of music and like to play basketball together.*

Tom, age sixteen[2]

*A lot of my closest friends I've known since the 5th grade. We have a good time together going to the mall and hanging out at each other's houses. We all relate to each other really well.*

Jill, age fourteen[3]

Teens today will have many friendships throughout their lives. Friendships that start in kindergarten and last through high school and beyond may not be as common in today's mobile world as they used to be. Some friendships may fizzle out at the end of a school year, while others grow over time through all kinds of changes. But regardless of when a friendship is formed, or how long it lasts, having friends is an important and rewarding part of life. And some friendships become part of the story of your life.

*Friendships between young children typically do not last a lifetime, but it is possible.*

Friendships are such an everyday part of our lives that it can be easy to take them for granted. Having and keeping a good friend is a commitment of time and effort. Yet typically, the more time people spend together, the greater the chance for conflicts to arise. But conflicts are not always a reason to end a friendship. Conflicts give us the opportunity to communicate and find ways to get along better with a friend.

Some conflicts in friendships are unhealthy. Friendships that involve verbal or physical abuse, pressure to do something inappropriate, or threats are not healthy or safe. These kinds of friendships should be ended.

According to Dr. Robin Beach, professor of adolescent medicine at the University of Colorado School of Medicine and editor of *TeenGrowth.com*, friendships serve many purposes at each stage of a young person's life. Young children's friendships are usually based on having someone to play with. Teens prefer hanging out with a group of people that dress alike, listen to the same music, and/or share an interest in a sport or hobby, even if the interest is as simple as hanging out at the mall.[4]

As preteens enter middle school their friendships become a central part of their lives, and their circle of friends usually expands and changes. New friendships start to form (and old ones are continued) based on developing interests. In addition, many teens begin to want more out of their friendships than just a shared love of an activity.

Most teens want to hang out with people who like to do the same things and who also share the same opinions about things like doing drugs, dating, or the importance of school. And, because of all these new preferences, some friendships that started in elementary school may end.

| *Verbal Abuse Includes:* | *Physical Abuse Includes:* |
| --- | --- |
| ▱ Put-downs | ▱ Hitting |
| ▱ Humiliation | ▱ Kicking |
| ▱ Cursing | ▱ Shoving |
| ▱ Inappropriate sexual comments | ▱ Unwanted sexual touching |

*In middle school it was all about trying to fit in. I don't even think about it in high school. I just go with my friends. Sixth grade was pretty much when I got with my group of friends.*

Ryan, age sixteen[5]

*Our group started basically because sports and classes brought us together. Then we started having sleepovers that were all seven of us. We're not superficial, we're all a lot alike in the way we value school and think about our friendships.*

Marissa, age seventeen[6]

*Friendships can turn up where they are least expected—like in a study group or at the library.*

## Types of Friends

The word "friend" means different things to different people. Some teens consider a teammate a close friend. Other teens might refer to close friends as people they confide in and spend lots of time with.

Friendships can generally be placed into three categories: close or best friends, situational friends, and casual friends. Close or best friends spend a great deal of time together, share similar interests and beliefs, and support one another.

Some people have one best friend, and others have several close friends who are part of a group of friends.

Situational friends are people brought together regularly for a scheduled activity, like members of a study group, teammates, or neighborhood friends. If the friendship continues long after the initial situation ends, these types of friends may become close or best friends.[7]

Casual friends spend a limited amount of time with each other, like a friend of a friend, someone a teen chats with on the Internet, or a person who sits in the next row in class.

## Traits of a Good Friend

- Listens to and respects your point of view, even if he or she has a different one
- Is committed to being there in good times and in bad
- Can be trusted to keep a confidence and not talk about you behind your back
- Is fun to spend time with and shares your passion for an interest or hobby
- Is someone you enjoy being around
- Shares many of your values
- Is honest with you about how he or she feels about the friendship
- Is one of your biggest fans—recognizes your good qualities and weaknesses and likes you for who you are

Good friends are a great source of support to a teen struggling at school or home. Many times a friend is going through some of the same challenges at the same time, and will understand what another friend is feeling.

# 2

# Making Friends

**M**aking friends is something people do throughout their lives, sometimes without little thought to the process. New friends are made (and needed) almost every time a person begins a new school, new job, new place to live, or just a new stage in life. At the same time, it is important to maintain the friendships that are based on more than going to the same school or being on the same team.

> *There were a group of seven of us in the 6th grade and six of them moved away, so I was all alone again in the 7th grade. I started over and just talked to anyone I wanted to. By now I've made friends and am popular and people approach me. I didn't try too hard to make friends; I just talked to people.*
>
> Pat, age fourteen[1]

Making friends can seem a lot easier when five things are kept in mind:

1. **Slow and Steady Wins a Friend**

   Developing a close friendship usually takes a big dose of patience. Teens expecting to meet someone and instantly become best friends will be quickly frustrated. Friendships typically develop over lots of chats, get-togethers, and events. Friendships naturally evolve when a person relaxes and focuses on meeting and getting to know people rather than searching for the "perfect" friend.

2. **Design a Friend**

   Some people find it helpful to make a list of things important to them in a friendship by thinking about what they liked best in previous friendships. Teens should avoid desperate attempts to do anything in exchange for a friendship. For example, they should not get involved in illegal activities, cut others down, or pretend to be something they are not.

3. **Nobody's Perfect**

   It is highly unlikely that any one person will share all of a teen's interests and attitudes. Most people have several close friends that they relate to for different reasons.

*I talk about guys and field hockey with one friend; another friend is the person I vent to about teachers and stuff; another is someone that looks just like me so we joke that we're twins; and another was my first friend from when I moved here in the 3rd grade.*

Marissa, age seventeen[2]

## 4. The Bad News/Good News

No matter who a person is, or how popular, there will be others who dislike him or her. This fact is hard to swallow at any age. It is kind of like music. Everyone has a type of music or a favorite group he or she relates to. And there are fans out there for all types of music. It is the same with people. Everyone has preferences for certain types of people.

Liking or disliking someone else has just as much to do with the person doing the liking as it does with the person being liked. The only thing people can control is whom they choose to like and how they treat other people. And it is important that all people treat others with respect whether or not they like them.

## 5. Some People Just Have the Gift of Gab

Outgoing people are great at starting conversations and inviting people to get together, whereas shy people struggle to get that first sentence out. Shy people can be awesome friends, too. They just need to work harder to overcome their hesitations and start talking to people.

## How to Make New Friends

*I have recently gotten to be really good friends with Cari—we go to the same school, and we have dance together—so we are with each other almost 24/7.*

**Katie, age fifteen**[3]

*I met Anthony through basketball at the YMCA. Our dads became friends too, and then we all saw each other all the time.*

**Ryan, age sixteen**[4]

The best place to meet new friends is in a place or group made up of people who like to do the same things. Sports teams, YMCAs, teen centers, musical groups, community or religious organizations, and school clubs are all excellent examples of places to meet people easily.

Other ways to meet people are by starting a conversation with someone else while walking to school or sitting in the next row in class. All it takes is two people in the same place at the same time.

Lots of people (including many adults) feel nervous starting a conversation with a stranger. Instead of worrying about how to walk up to someone and say, "Hey, do you want to be my friend?" try to focus on starting one short conversation. Be curious and observant—What would be interesting to know about this person? What seems likeable about him or her? Ask questions about what you want to know.

Looks alone are not a good indicator of whether or not someone would be a good friend. In fact, many people find that an average-looking person becomes much more attractive once they get to know him or her. And an attractive person who is a snob can seem less attractive.

## Moving and Making New Friends

*Don't be so concerned about making friends right away, just observe people and see who you think would be nice. Even though it's hard to feel like you don't have any friends, if you*

## *How to Talk to a Possible Friend:*

"Did you get the homework assignment last night?"

"How do you think you did on last week's test?"

"Hi, I think we live in the same neighborhood. I live on Parkwood Street. Where do you live?"

"I hear you're new here, too. Where did you live before?"

"I'm thinking of joining the drama club. You're a member, right? Have you liked the club?"

"I heard tryouts are next week for the JV team—are you trying out?"

### How to say it:

The way something is said is almost as important as what is said. A friendly, confident tone (regardless of how you might be feeling on the inside) is more likely to start a conversation.

### When:

If possible, a teen should approach the person he or she would like to get to know when the person is alone. This reduces the chance of being embarrassed in front of a bunch of people and increases the chance of a friendly response.

### Follow-up:

After a few short conversations, ask the person if he or she would like to walk to school together, go to a game, or hang out together. If the person says "no," but you have the feeling he or she might want to get together at another time, wait a few days and ask to do something else. In the meantime, make sure to keep talking to others too.

### Do not give up:

Even if nothing comes out of several attempts, the important thing to remember is that the only failure is not to try. It takes courage to put oneself out there and take chances, and that is something to feel proud of regardless of the initial outcome. If a person chooses not to be friends with you, try not to think of it as being rejected—after all, how can they be rejecting you if they do not even know you?[5] And, as Dr. Beach has found, "for every good friendship we have there are going to be three or four that don't work out."[6]

*rush into making friends you could easily end up with the wrong ones.*

Marissa, age seventeen[7]

*I was lucky when I moved because this kid came up to me and introduced himself. We had a lot in common. From there I met his group and then branched off from there.*

Pat, age fourteen[8]

Moving to a new place can make even the most confident teens wonder if something is wrong with them. Everyone may seem so different from the people in the old school. It can be hard not to focus on all of the differences because moving makes everything different. Neighborhoods, schools, houses, and routines all change.

The best way to make friends in a new place is to be nice to everyone and not make friends exclusively with any one person. This gives the new person time to figure out the various groups, what they are all about, and what the people in them are like. Remember to smile at people when they make eye contact. Say "Hi, what's up?"

In the meantime, teens will feel less lonely if they keep talking to old friends on the phone and visiting them, if possible.

## Boys and Girls Have Different Types of Friendships

According to Dr. Beach, both boys and girls make friends to help them break away from family and identify with peers. However, friendships between boys usually center on activities, such as playing computer games or baseball. Girls tend to look for friends that will enhance their self-image, and for people to share their fears and dreams with.

*Girls often bond by talking and sharing, while boys often form friendships through shared activities.*

Girls tend to get closer emotionally because they often spend hours talking and sharing their private thoughts and feelings. That is why girls tend to define a good friend as someone who understands their feelings.[9]

In middle school, girls can easily become jealous of their closest friends, but high school girls are typically more tolerant of their friends and their differences. This is most likely because, toward the end of high school, girls are more confident in themselves and less fearful of being betrayed or deserted by their friends. They begin to understand that a friend can have close relationships with others without it always being a threat to their friendship.[10]

Boys are more likely to keep sensitive information private, and instead prefer friends who they can trust to stick by them when another boy threatens them. If boys do share their feelings, it is usually with a trusted female friend. Boys also tend to hang out in groups based on what they do together instead of shared feelings.[11]

## Can Guys and Girls Be Friends?

*Guy friends can give you advice that girl friends can't. They give great guy advice and they also tend to be less judgmental than girls.*

Katie, age fifteen[12]

*My best friend is a girl. People always think we're going out but we're not. The guys give me a hard time sometimes because I hang out with girls, but I probably know more about girls than anyone else in my school. Now guys come to me for advice about girls they like.*

Jason, age fifteen[13]

Friendships between guys and girls are a lot of fun and have many advantages. Having a friend of the opposite sex is a great way to get a perspective on how the other "half" of the population looks at things. It is also a reminder that people are people whether they are male or female. Both boys and girls can be great, assertive, sensitive, caring, and fun to be with.

Also, having several friends of the opposite sex helps teens determine what is important to them in future romantic relationships. Sometimes friendships turn into a dating relationship. If both of the friends want to start

*Friendships between guys and girls bring a new perspective and insight that is not usually gained by only having friends of the same sex.*

dating each other, they usually have a good foundation for their relationship because of their friendship.

However, if only one person has a crush on the other, the friendship could be at risk. Before a teen pursues a romantic relationship with a friend, he or she should think about the possibility of remaining friends should the other person not have the same feelings.

If it is difficult to figure out if a friend is interested in a romantic relationship, try asking an indirect question like, "Isn't it weird how everyone thinks we're going out because we're always together?" Or try asking the friend directly by saying, "We're such great friends, do you think we'd make a good couple too?" Or put out a feeler like, "Katie thinks we might as well be going out because of all the time we spend together. I wonder what it would be like if we were."

Alternately, if one friend wants to start dating the other, and that person does not want to start dating, it is best for the friend to talk about it. Try saying something like "I feel so flattered that you like me in that way. I like you a lot, too, but in a friend way. We have so much fun together. I would hate for us to start going out and ruin our friendship. I think it would be hard to go back to being great friends if we dated, and I don't want to lose our friendship."

# 3

# The Three P's—
# Peer Pressure, Popularity,
# and Parents

*I didn't like feeling pressured by my friends. It just made me confused about what I really wanted. I couldn't separate their feelings from my true feelings to tell what I wanted. I didn't really say anything to my friends about this because I really didn't know what to say.*

Katie, age fifteen[1]

No one gets to skip life's class on peer pressure. Every teen experiences it throughout adolescence, with a few surprises. The first surprise is that peer pressure is not all bad. Positive peer pressure can motivate teens to work harder in school, play better in a game, work at a problem, and set goals.

The second thing to consider is that peer pressure goes both ways. People will pressure others as well as be pressured. Every teen is capable of having a good or bad influence on his or her friends.

In addition, when people pick a friend or group of friends they choose the type of peer pressure they will live with. When a teen befriends a group that uses drugs, that teen will be offered drugs. When a teen's friends are working hard at school, he or she will most likely be motivated to work hard too.[2]

> *I'm pretty lucky. I fell into a group that really doesn't care what each of us does. My friends are understanding and respect other people.*
>
> Tom, age sixteen[3]

*Negative peer pressure can be hard to resist. But with the right friends to support you, it can be easy to say "no."*

**Negative Peer Pressure Includes:**
- Pressure to take drugs and/or drink
- Pressure to have sex if you are not ready for it
- Pressure to date the "right" person
- Pressure to skip classes and/or do poorly in school
- Pressure to mistreat others
- Pressure to get in a fight with someone else

Peer pressure is usually strongest around age eleven because most middle schoolers are looking for a safety net at this stage. At this age teens no longer want to be dependent on parents, yet they do not yet have the skills or confidence to be independent. Many crave the support of friends as they make the transition to their late teens.[4] By the time a teen is graduating from high school, he or she is usually more confident in his or her identity and able to get along with a greater variety of people.

What one friend thinks of another seems so important at this stage that it can be hard to resist peer pressure. Negative peer pressure is a test of a teen's values and his or her ability to stand up for them.

Parents can give teens tons of rules—sometimes going along with peers seems like a way of getting away from adult rules. Yet, it is important for teens to respect their parents, as well as make some of their own rules. Here are some examples:

- How long do I think I should know or date someone before we kiss?
- What kind of touching bothers me?
- What do I honestly think about doing drugs?
- How do I really want to do in school, and how will that affect my future?

Once teens have made rules for themselves, they can imagine how they would handle situations where they would be pressured to violate their own rules. Teens who successfully resist peer pressure usually have several things in common: an inner sense of what is important, self-confidence, a belief that it is okay to be unique, and an ability to communicate well with friends.

These teens are able to see and avoid certain risks like getting into a car with someone who has been drinking. For others, it may take a tragedy to see the reality of the consequences. Sometimes a teen has only a few seconds to make a tough decision that could have life-or-death consequences.[5]

The choices teens make either prove that they can stay true to themselves, or that they have given control over their decisions to someone else.

It is hard to say "no" when it seems everyone else is doing it. It takes a confident person to say "no" to his or her friends or the popular people. It is difficult not to worry what others will say, or worse, about being excluded from a group. But, it is also a great way to find out who your real friends are. Here are some things teens can ask, say, and do when they are feeling pressured:

### When faced with pressure, ask these questions:

"Will this affect the goals I have set for myself?"
"How will I feel about myself if I give in?"
"Will I still respect myself if I do this?"
"Why am I considering going along?"
"Who is in control of who I want to be?"[6]

*Most people are cool. If they offer you something and you say no they don't keep bugging you. It's your choice.*

*Jason, age fifteen*[7]

***What to say when feeling pressured:***

"No thanks, but you can if you want to."

"Hey, if you were really my friend you would not keep bothering me to do this. You would respect my opinion."

"Do not touch me there!"

"I have asthma, I really cannot smoke."

***What to do:***

Walk away

Push the person's hand away

Call someone for help

Leave and say you have to be someplace in a few minutes

Avoid a situation you know will be tough to get out of

When possible, think of your options before getting into a situation

Even though people have no control over what someone else might say, do, or think about them, people can control what they do and how they think about themselves. Do not give that control away!

Teens who believe that it is okay to be unique or different usually have an easier time resisting peer pressure. According to a *Newsweek* poll, when teens age thirteen to nineteen were asked, "If you had to choose between fitting in with friends or becoming outstanding in some way, which would you choose?" Twenty-six percent of teens chose "fitting in" and 69 percent chose "becoming outstanding."[8] What matters is not whether or not a teen is pressured, but what each teen chooses to do about the pressure. As the *Newsweek* poll showed, many teens would prefer to be true to their values and interests.

## *Popularity*

The belief that popular teens are somehow better than everyone else is false. Friendly and interesting people can be found in groups considered popular as well as unpopular. Certain groups seem to rank higher on the popularity ladder than others, yet what really matters is being popular within whatever group a teen belongs to.

All popular kids are not the same. Some popular teens act like they are better than everyone else. Usually these teens are popular not because of their good qualities, but because they are part of an "in" group, or are beautiful or rich. Others are great people who show respect for everyone.

> *Lots of people in my school who are popular have an attitude and focus mostly on looks and clothes. I've always kind of been with the popular crowd, but I'm starting to notice that they talk behind each other's back–and you always have to try to be something you're not. It's not fun. My closest friends aren't like that; they're fun to be around.*
>
> Jill, age fourteen[9]

Popularity in the early teen years may seem critically important. "Am I popular?" may be a young teen's first identity crisis as he or she starts to look for reasons why he or she is popular or unpopular. Older teens may wonder "Who am I?" and "Where am I headed?"[10]

There is a difference between being well known and well liked. The traits that make someone genuinely popular are usually the same throughout life. Truly popular people are typically friendly, helpful, sociable, confident, and they usually do not focus on being popular. Genuinely popular people usually focus on what interests them, like school clubs or activities, sports, volunteering, or basically anything that makes them feel good about themselves.

*I used to think it was looks that made some people popular but I got away from that. Somebody bold, original, willing to do their own thing and willing to stand out and not really care what others think—that's popular.*

Tom, age sixteen[11]

*Being popular is just being outgoing, not caring who you talk to, just being friends with everybody and hanging out with your group.*

Ryan, age sixteen[12]

Some unpopular teens (even within a popular group) are aggressive, cruel, or mean-spirited. Others are conceited, self-centered, defensive, or just not fun to be around.

Some teens place little value on being popular; others consider it crucial to being happy. Many teens are surprised to find that being in the popular group does not provide the security they had hoped for. In fact, many people in popular groups actually feel more insecure as they constantly struggle to do the "right thing" to stay in the group.

The most important thing is how a teen feels with the friends he or she has even if that means being popular in an unpopular group.

*I strive to be popular among my own friends. If I am well liked among my friends, that's all that matters!*

Katie, age fifteen[13]

## Parents and Friends

Parents sometimes feel like outsiders as their children naturally start to spend increasing amounts of time with friends and less time with family. Or, at the very least, parents may worry about what teens are doing with all the

*Talking to parents and discussing their concerns can resolve a lot of issues. It can help make them more comfortable about trusting your judgment.*

time they spend with friends. From the parents' point of view, their teen dresses differently, speaks a language they do not understand, and starts to have viewpoints they may not share. Sometimes parents react by making more restrictions.

### *Tips for Improving Relationships With Parents:*

- Acknowledge parents' concerns, whether it is about going to a party or missing a class. Listen to why they are worried and tell them how you plan to make a responsible decision.
- Ask your parents questions about clothes they wore and things they did in school.

- If your parents dislike your friend(s), ask them why. Maybe all you need to do is let your parents get to know your friends better. Also ask, "Is there something I do or say when I am with that friend that you don't like?"
- Turn to your parents with a problem. If you talk to your parents about problems you have, or about problems you have had and how you have worked them out on your own, you show them you can handle teenage challenges—and will turn to them for help when you need to.
- Try sharing a movie or music that you really like with them and tell them what you like about it.

Usually, the more times a teen has proven to be honest, trustworthy, and good at making responsible decisions, the more opportunities parents will give the teen to make these decisions.

# 4

# Dealing With Conflicts

All friendships are guaranteed to go through difficult times. The good news is conflicts can actually make a friendship stronger when friends work through them together. They are not always the end of a friendship.

Conflicts are a sure thing because no two people like, dislike, and believe in the exact same things, and these likes and dislikes usually change over time. Conflicts in friendships can result from small misunderstandings, like a, forgotten phone call, or they can be major conflicts, like, when one friend reveals another friend's secret.

Everybody has to overcome at least a few of these obstacles in their friendships. When these issues are considered part of friendship, instead of as a failure of some sort, teens are better prepared to work through the bumpy spots of relating to other people.

*About five of us (friends) tried out for the cheerleading squad. Three of us made it, and two did not. We found out one of the*

## Issues That Can Cause Conflicts in a Friendship:

- Misunderstandings
- Rumors
- New people that come into a friendship
- One friend feels pressured by another
- Pressure to ignore other friends
- Secrets revealed (trust broken)
- Boyfriend/girlfriend issues
- Personal struggles with health, family, or school

*girls didn't care if she made it or not and got over it in a couple of days. The other girl ended up saying that cheerleading was the stupidest sport ever created and that she was happy that she didn't make it because it was just a waste of time. This made us feel our accomplishment hadn't been such a great thing after all. I thought about this for a while and realized that she was so hurt, sad, and frustrated that this was her way of making herself feel better.*

Samantha, age fourteen[1]

Conflicts are opportunities to understand oneself and a friend better. It takes a lot of practice to learn to express anger, hurt, and disappointment without blaming or being overly critical. Resorting to physical or mental abuse of others, or yourself, is *never* a healthy response.

## Arguments and Fights

Often fights begin with rude remarks. Sometimes it can help to respond nicely, as if the person had not been rude at all. Or teens can try to defuse the situation by asking questions, using humor, or acting as if the other person really meant it as a compliment. Examples include:

*Stay clam, ask questions, and try to understand the other person's point of view:*

- "I'm sorry, I didn't know that bothered you. There is a nicer way you can let me know you're angry about it."
- "Is everything okay at home?"
- "I didn't realize that hurt you, is there something we can do so this isn't a problem anymore?"

*Try to make a joke out of the comment:*

- "I wonder when you'll find a new hobby to replace harassing me."
- "I didn't realize you already had a degree in fashion."
- "Oh thank you for that great advice."[2]

If the person does not let up it is best to ignore the tirade and walk away. Say something like "Seems like now is not a good time for us to talk, I'll give you a call later on when we are both calm and can talk."

Some people find it hard to stop at a few angry comments and walk away. If a lot of people are present when a fight seems to be brewing, many times the spectators will make it worse by encouraging the fight. But no matter how much pressure or momentum seems to be building toward a fight, each person can always choose to walk away.

## Being in the Middle of Two Arguing Friends

When two friends are arguing it can be hard to stay out of the middle of it. When a teen wants to remain friends with both people, the best thing to do is stay neutral and stop talking about one friend with the other. Tell both friends how important they are and express concern at being put in the middle of the situation. Try to understand each friend's position without trying to get him or her to understand the other.

## When a Best Friend Makes a New Close Friend

It can be hard not to be jealous when a friend starts spending time with another friend. It is not necessarily the end of the friendship. People can have many friendships, each one close in a different way.

There is an ebb and flow to friendships. When a friend is spending time with another person, it is best for the "outside" friend to explore other friendships or interests until the friend gravitates back. A true friend does not try to control another friend's relationships with other people.[3]

## What Will My Friends Think if I Hang Out With This Person?

Popular teens sometimes worry about how their group will react if they spend time with someone considered unpopular. It is important to remember that all people have the right, and the choice, to spend time with people they like, regardless of the person's popularity status.

## Secrets Revealed, or Broken Trust

Revealing a friend's secret, taking something from a friend, or saying something hurtful behind a friend's back are all things that can break trust in a friendship. Teens in this situation should acknowledge what happened and apologize.

The friendship may still end, but if an apology is not made, the chances of saving the friendship are slim. If the friendship ends anyway, the best thing a teen can do is remember that all people make mistakes and try to learn from the experience.

Good friends will not believe bad things said about a friend without checking with him or her first. If the person being talked about knows who is spreading the rumors, he or she can try saying something, like "I've heard you've been saying things that aren't true about me. Why are you doing that?"[4] Or, "Do you really believe what you are saying or are you trying to hurt me?" And, "I know you are a better person than to say things that aren't true."

> *When I got in a fight with one of my friends, she tried to make all of my other friends hate me. Luckily, I have awesome friends and they didn't believe her. Those friends helped me through the bad time, and I learned who my true friends really are.*
>
> Katie, age fifteen[5]

## Using People Does Not Equal Friendship

Solid friendships are not built on someone using his or her friends. Some teens think other people exist for copying homework, borrowing money, providing rides, or just gaining access to a desired group. There is a big difference between sharing and using. When friends share with each other, things go two ways—each person shares his or her resources or talents with the other. Using is when one person befriends another only to get something he or she wants.

If a teen wants to figure out if they are being used, they can stop providing the thing they think they are being used for and see if the friendship continues. For example, if the person does not want to spend time with a friend because the friend no longer gives him or her a ride to school, that will tell a lot about the friendship.[6]

## Silence Between Friends

When a teen does not know why a friend seems to have dumped him or her, he or she should approach the person and say, "It seems like something is wrong between us. Can you tell me what has changed?" If the person refuses to talk—or worse yet, ignores the friend even more—then that person is not being a good friend.

In addition, if a teen has done something to contribute to the hostility in the friendship, even if it is not the main issue, he or she should apologize. Apologizing lets friends know that their hurt has been understood, and usually reunites friends through understanding.

*Right now I'm annoyed with a friend and I haven't said anything yet, but I know I should talk it out. I know if you don't talk to a person you just get madder and madder and start to hate them so you don't want to talk to them anymore.*

Marissa, age seventeen[7]

When people truly care about their friends, they try to accept them as they grow and change. For example, changes in a friendship are almost guaranteed when young teens are thrown in with lots of new people at the start of middle school. When confronted with these changes, teens must ask themselves questions, like "Just because we don't live near each other anymore am I willing to let this relationship go?" or "Now that my friend, left the soccer team, do I consider her less of a friend, or do I want to look for other ways for us to spend time together?"

*When teens are concerned about a friend, talking to an adult may not seem like the best idea. Sometimes, though, it can save a friendship—or even a life.*

### How To Minimize Conflicts:

- Tell the truth.
- Never tell a friend's secret, unless they are in danger.
- Support a friend in his or her new interest, even if you do not share that interest.
- Do not tell a friend something bad another friend said about him or her.
- Do not pressure a friend to do something he or she does not want to do.
- Do not take advantage of friends by constantly asking for rides, or borrowing clothes or money,

especially if they do not ever offer these things to you.

- Turn to a trusted adult for help when a conflict seems impossible to resolve.
- Immediately seek out an adult if there is any type of abuse involved.

*I've started telling my older sister and my mom some of my problems. I know they're not going to go and tell the friend I have a problem with about it.*

Marissa, age seventeen[8]

An adult can help a teen figure out what factors are within his or her control and what ones are not. Together they can discuss possible choices, what they will mean, and how they can be communicated.

## Friends in Trouble

An important part of friendship is helping a friend through a difficult time. Lots of people have emotional difficulties because of issues or events such as:

- Moving
- Parents' divorce
- Sexual pressure from boyfriend/girlfriend
- Illness in the family or in themselves
- Death of a family member or friend
- Eating disorders
- Drinking or drug problems
- Depression

While a good friend should be there for his or her friend, serious problems need much more help than one teen can provide. Try talking to your friend alone. Say something like, "I'm worried about you, you seem so sad all the time," or "You seem to be drinking a lot. Is everything okay?"

Chances are good that he or she may not respond positively to your concerns. But true friends care so much about a friend's physical and mental health that they will risk the friendship to get help for their friend. The friend of someone who is troubled can talk to a parent, a trusted teacher, or a guidance counselor. And remember, only the person in the situation is responsible for the choices he or she is making. Only that person can start choosing differently once help is given. No matter how much they may care, one person can not force another to change if the person chooses not to.

# 5

# Cliques

*The "posers" all wear surfer clothes and brand names. They really think they're better than all of us. But we (punkers) are cool too, but different.*

Jason, age fifteen[1]

*I have a lot of friends in different groups, but I guess people see me as a headbanger. We listen to rock and stuff. I don't like the name, but it's the music I listen to and I'm not ashamed of it. A lot of groups I notice are because they listen to the same type of music.*

Pat, age fourteen[2]

*I think everyone is "labeled" and it can be hard to get a new one. Sometimes it bothers me that people just categorize me as one thing, but I usually don't care. My true friends know who I really am and they don't care about that label.*

Katie, age fifteen[3]

Recognize any of these? Goths, grungers, alternatives, skaters, jocks, headbangers, druggies, preps, posers, rednecks—thcy are all examples of cliques or groups of teens that have a shared identity.

Most members of cliques see themselves as distinctly different from others and go to great lengths to be similar to one another within their group. Usually members will dress the same, listen to the same music, and have words whose meanings are only known to fellow group members.[4] In addition, there is the proverbial "popular group" that is based more on the mysteries of looks, athletic skill, charm, and wealth than identity.[5]

Clique labels are stereotypes. Some teens like being identified by a group label; others find it hurtful and limiting, especially those who did not have a choice in their label or get a negative label. Cliques can prevent people from learning about others and their points of view. And, whether someone likes their label or not, it can be very difficult to change it without changing schools.

> *My school is known for their cliques. My last school had your typical cliques, but my high school now also has culture cliques like the Mexicans, Asians, Portuguese–that sort of thing.*
>
> Jason, age fifteen[6]

## Some Reasons Why Teens Belong to Cliques:

- Popularity
- Safety and security
- Shared interests
- Image
- Sense of belonging
- To have fun

Being part of a large group of friends can have many benefits. At the same time, teens have to remember not to lose their identity within the group.

Teens belong to groups or cliques for a variety of reasons. Being in a group tends to be critically important to someone in early adolescence because many ten- to fourteen-year-olds crave the sense of security a group provides. Usually as teens reach the end of high school, they are more confident about themselves and less dependent on a group for approval.[7]

Having a large group of friends can be a good experience. A great group of friends can provide support, buddies who share an interest, a sense of security, and fun. Groups of friends can be unhealthy or even dangerous if a teen loses his or her sense of self and ability to make good decisions.

> *One friend I had did everything she could to be in the "in" group; she was obsessed with being popular. If she said she liked a type of music and then someone said they didn't like it she would automatically say "oh, well I really don't like it that much either."*
>
> Jason, age fifteen[8]

## Being Excluded from a Clique

> *I wanted to hang out with these people who were from a different middle school and they didn't even give me a chance. They already had a clique from the previous years so I ignored it and went on with my life.*
>
> Samantha, age fourteen[9]

Being excluded from a desired group can be difficult to handle. It is hard not to take it personally. Often, though, it has nothing to do with the person being excluded and everything to do with the established bond between the existing group members, as Samantha discovered.

Other times a teen is left out for no apparent reason or for something superficial such as what he or she wore on a particular day. Cliques can be verbally and/or physically cruel to people outside of their group, which can lead to fights and/or competition between groups.

Some teens will harass others in front of their friends, by teasing them about their weight, clothes, grades, or basically anything that will make the tormenter look "cool" in front of his or her friends. Even if a group says nothing to an individual, sometimes staring alone is enough to intimidate and hurt the person who has been left out.

### Tips for Handling Being Excluded:

1. Do not be a "wannabe." If a group excludes you, start making contact with others. Eventually you will find a group of friends who appreciate you.

2. Think about your own interests, likes, and dislikes. Look for others who share your beliefs and goals instead of trying to be something you are not.

3. Think about the advantages and disadvantages of the clique. People in groups based on their real identities are often more content than teens in the "popular" group.[10]

4. Accept yourself even if no one else does. You may have a hidden talent or be more mature or serious than others your age. Bill Gates, Christina Aguilera, Nick Carter of the Backstreet Boy's, and some famous movie stars all admit they were outcasts in high school.[11]

## How to Know When It Is Time to Leave a Clique

Life can be difficult even for those teens accepted into a clique. If the group constantly makes judgments about its members' actions, appearances, and dating choices, it can become hard for a person to figure out what he or she really

*Teens who feel excluded from a clique can find positive ways to handle the hurt. One way is to get involved in new activities that the clique members are not involved in.*

wants to do in a situation, as opposed to what fellow group members think the person should do. This pressure usually comes from the group's fears of people who do things differently or have different values.

Or it could be because the group members have too high an opinion of themselves and simply look down on anyone different and on anyone who does not conform to their ideas of what makes a person worthy. When any of these things start to happen, it is in a teen's best interest to find other friends.

## Reasons a Young Person Would or Should Leave a Clique:

1. You are getting a bad reputation, or are being labeled as someone who does something you do not really want to do.
2. The group tries to restrict friendships with people outside of the group.
3. You feel exhausted or stressed out from trying to "keep up" with the group.
4. Your "friends" are punishing you by ignoring you, calling you names, or being hurtful in some way as payback for not going along with the group.
5. You prefer just to have a few close friendships.
6. It is not fun anymore.

A teen should never accept physical or sexual abuse from a clique. Any type of assualt or sexual abuse is serious and should be talked about and reported immediately to a trusted adult. Reporting it is the best chance to stop it. If abuse is not reported, it almost always continues—if not with you, then with some other victim.

When a teen decides to leave a clique, he or she has a few options for getting out. Teens with a variety of friends outside of their main group have an easier time moving away from a bad group of friends to better friendships with others.

*Everyone seems to be in his or her own little group. I was trying this year to get to know people that before I thought were a little weird, but then I got to know them and thought they were cool. Actually, we had a lot in common.*

Jill, age fourteen[12]

The slow and easy way out of a group is to gradually spend less time with the current group and more time with new friends. It is easier to leave a group if a teen has at least one friend that he or she can count on. However, if a group is being abusive, it is important to get as much distance from the group as possible immediately, and seek help from a trusted adult.

Sometimes it is impossible to leave a group without someone asking for an explanation. A respectful explanation will decrease the chances of starting a fight with former friends. The teen wanting to leave could say something like, "Now that I'm not on the team anymore I feel more comfortable hanging out with these guys." Or, "I really like the people I've met working on the school play and we've just been hanging out a lot more together."

No matter what the group members say, avoid criticizing the group. Moving on takes courage, and the reward for that courage will be better friendships, and a smarter, more confident self.

No matter what group someone is in, good group members are those who know how to empathize with, understand, and listen to others. They are people who consider how their actions and words will affect other people. And they accept others who are different from them.

Keep in mind that there is no rule against starting a group of friends. Every person is in charge of who his or her friends are and of making new ones. It is not about how many friends someone has, but how a person feels around the friends he or she does have.

# 6

# How to Deal With Former Friends and Bullies

*My friend and I became friends with another girl and then the two of them started telling secrets and planning to go on spring break together. They ended up becoming best friends and pushing me out.*

Marissa, age seventeen[1]

*A couple of years ago I had a friendship end. I broke off the friendship because as I got to know her better, I found out that the girl wasn't the type of person that I wanted to be around. She started hanging out with people who got drunk a lot and did drugs. They had a bad influence on her personality.*

Katie, age fifteen[2]

*Everyone just doesn't go up to each other and say "We have to get this kid out of the group." We didn't have to verbally say it, everyone just kind of distanced themselves from him. He just did stupid stuff.*

Pat, age fourteen[3]

Some friendships gradually fade as two people go in opposite directions, develop new interests, and have different schedules. Other times friendships end bitterly for a variety of reasons, or abruptly for no apparent reason. No matter how a friendship ends, losing a friend is a hard thing to experience. And it can be even harder if that friend starts to bully his or her former friend.

Depending on the circumstance, a teen can end a friendship in a number of ways. Some friendships fizzle out if both people start to be less available to one another and more available to others who share new interests, classes, or values. If each friend makes the transition smoothly, confrontations and arguments can be avoided.

*A lot of my friendships ended because we weren't in the same school or classes anymore. Another friendship ended because*

## How to Know When a Friendship Is Nearing the End:

- You no longer feel like you can trust your friend.
- You feel uncomfortable or angry around your friend.
- Your friend teases, gossips about you, or belittles you.
- Your friend is never there for you when you need him or her.
- Your friend does not respect your preferences in other friends, music, or clothes.
- You dread seeing your friend and start avoiding his or her calls or spending time with him or her, or you think your friend may be feeling that way about you.
- Other people begin to warn you about your friend
- Each of you seems to be going in opposite directions and spending increasing amounts of time on separate interests.

*we both just seemed to change or mature differently. We never really talked about it. We each just started doing our own thing and we went from being best friends to just friends.*

Jill, age fourteen[4]

Many times friendship breakups are more difficult. Sometimes one friend wants to keep the friendship going and is hurt that the other does not.

## What to Do When Breaking Off a Friendship

Most people are tempted to avoid the awkward experience of telling a friend that the friendship is over. It seems easier to avoid the person or to make excuses for not getting together. People often convince themselves that not only is this easier for them, but it is also easier on the friend to "let them down easy." However, people can be hurt more when friends pretend that everything is fine, then suddenly dump them. It can help if they know up front that a friendship is ending and why.[5]

Teens that want to end a friendship could say something like "I'm having a hard time telling you this because you've been a great friend and the last thing I want to do is hurt your feelings. But I just don't feel the same anymore about our friendship. It's just that I've changed and I feel more comfortable hanging out with the people I've met in the band. I'm just not into the soccer team the way I used to be."

Teens worried about a friend who starts to use drugs or is spending time with a new clique could approach their friend and say, "We've been friends for such a long time it's hard for me to see our friendship coming to an end. But, I'm not comfortable with the people you've started to hang out with. The stuff you guys do scares me and just doesn't feel right for me so I need to stop hanging out with you."

It is hard to predict how friends will react when a friendship breaks up, and it is normal for both people to feel bad. It is also normal for the friend being "dumped" to feel angry at first. The best thing to do is give that person space to recover and make new friends. Try not to take angry feelings personally, act cruel, or get into a fight with the former friend.

As hard as it is to break off a friendship, it is even harder to be rejected by a friend. Many teens find it hard not to let what a former friend said about them affect their confidence. There are several things a teen can do to learn from a past friendship and move on to a better one.

## Things Not to Do to a Former Friend:

- Make harassing phone calls
- Attempt to physically hurt him or her
- Spread rumors about him or her
- Criticize or laugh at your former friend in front of other people

### What to Do When a Friend has Rejected You:

- Remember that everyone is worthy of a good friend. When people choose new friends it has just as much (if not more) to do with who they are than who the friend is. A teen is going to hang out with people that he or she can relate to. When rejected friends go on to find new friends, they often discover even better friendships.

- Do not chase after the person; try to accept it even if the ex-friend is unwilling to reveal what went wrong.

- Spend time with other people, whether they are family members, casual friends, or other people that seem interesting. Any of these can lead to new friendships.

- Pursue something that interests you that your old friend would never have tried.

- Do not say bad things about an ex-friend. The person spreading rumors looks just as bad as the person being talked about.

*Taking part in group activities is a great way to make new friends.*

## Surviving the Bullies

Sometimes, even when teens do the best they can to leave a group or a friend with dignity and respect, past friends can turn cruel and become enemies. Being bullied can make it unbearable to go to school or hang around at the same places.[6]

While teens have no control over what others will do or say about them, they can do things to lessen the effect an enemy has on them by avoiding contact and not getting caught in a bad-mouthing war with their former friends.

> *I wish that I had known sooner not to let people bother me too much because they are either jealous of you or trying to make you mad. The more you show people that they are bothering you and hurting your feelings, the more they will do it because then they feel cool and powerful. If you blow them off, they realize it isn't working.*
>
> Samantha, age fourteen[7]

The more attention teens give to negative things being said about them, the more they will provoke additional comments. Bullies feed on making other teens cry, cower, and fall apart. Refuse to give in to them. Think of it as starving them because the person being bullied is the one in control of whether or not the bully gets fed.[8]

The best revenge is being happy. Ignoring teens who try to hassle others and getting on with life is the best way to get over a friendship that has turned sour. When teens are comfortable with themselves and focus on whatever it is that makes them happy, hurtful ex-friends lose the power to make life miserable.

# 7

# High School Reunion— The Future Face of Teen Friendships

Many teens envision their friendships lasting forever. Friendships made in school can become lifelong friendships. However, it is unlikely that more than a few will last through adulthood. And the ones that do may not be the ones a teen would expect.

> The friendships I've kept since school are not necessarily the ones I would have predicted would make it this far. But I'm really grateful to have them. These are the people I can call up and say, "Remember so-and-so? Remember the time we...?" and they know exactly what I'm talking about. We can talk now about our jobs, our husbands, our kids, but we can just as easily slip back into high school memories and laugh.
>
> Jen, age thirty-three[1]

*Lifelong friendships can be a lot of work, but are worth the effort.*

What makes some friendships last through a lifetime of changes like moving away, college, careers, marriage, and starting families? Usually the friendships that make it do so because of shared histories, maybe a similar interest that has endured, good communication over time despite geographic separations, and most importantly, a commitment between friends to keep the friendship going.

*We (my three high school friends and I) have always said that we have made some great friends along the way from college, to jobs to hangouts, but no one will ever be like us. We know each other in ways people you meet when you're grown up will never know you. We knew each other when we were insecure competitive teens, belonging to intermingling cliques with bad perms and stupid boyfriends. We've seen each other grow up and we've grown very far apart at times. But we always come back full circle.*

Sue, age twenty-nine[2]

*I'm still friends with a girl I met my sophomore year in high school. Since college we've tried to get together at least once a month to hang out, watch a movie, or go out for a drink. When it comes to friends, you have to make the effort instead of putting it off so much. Kerry and I have been friends now for eight years and through our adventures, the obstacles we've faced, and the talks we've had, our friendship is still there and I love her to death.*

Lorrie, age twenty-three[3]

It is also important to remember that the pressure teens feel in middle and high school to have the "right" friends does not last. One of the great things about college, or life after high school, is each person gets the chance to reinvent himself or herself. The "in crowd" has to start all over again, cliques yield little power and influence, and people get to know each other more for who they are as opposed to what group they belong to, or what they have "heard through the grapevine" about a person.

*The friendships I have now I value 100 percent more than the ones I had in high school. My friends now are not out of convenience. I've met them all through mutual interests, some at work or some through friends of co-workers. They're all people I want to spend time with and we have a lot in common.*

Drew, age twenty-six[4]

*I'm closer with a friend from college because of the obstacles we've helped each other overcome. Even though we have our differences they are actually complementary and our core values are the same. I can just be my true self with her.*

Mary, age twenty-eight[5]

*Once I got away from this area it made me feel bad that my high school friends seemed like they were just going to sit around in their basements, smoking dope and just working to spend money on substance abuse or basically any form of short term gratification. They just seem stuck.*

Tom, age twenty-two[6]

One thing teens can look forward to (or dread) later in life is their high school reunions. Some people attend their reunion and find that people have not changed much. Others return and rekindle old friendships or start new ones with people they may not have given a second chance in high school.

*I'd have to say that I was most surprised (at my reunion) by how sweet some people were that I really never knew well in high school. I've rekindled some old friendships and started some new ones.*

Lauren, age thirty-three[7]

*I was nervous as anything, and almost copped out of attending my five-year reunion, but I learned a lot from going. I learned that time flies; it seems like just yesterday I was walking down the hallway of my high school with my books in one hand and a note to pass in the other. And I learned that my real friends were the ones I still wanted to keep in touch with five years after high school.*

Lorrie, age twenty-three[8]

Sometimes it is fun to think about what things will be like at that future reunion. "How will people remember me?" "Is there anyone I see around school that I could run into five or ten years later and think I wish I had taken the time to get to know that person better?" "Is there anything I've done, or am thinking of doing, that I'm sure I'll regret later on?" These are all good questions to think about while there is still a chance to make a change.

Each person has a lifetime to make great friendships. The best friendships are the ones that help us to find, and be true, to ourselves.

# Chapter Notes

## Chapter 1. What Is a Friend?

1. Interview with Katie, age 15, January 16, 2001.
2. Interview with Tom, age 16, January 25, 2001.
3. Interview with Jill, age 14, February 22, 2001.
4. Interview with Dr. Robin Beach, December 7, 2000.
5. Interview with Ryan, age 16, October 27, 2000.
6. Interview with Marissa (real name withheld for privacy), age 17, January 31, 2001.
7. Terri Apter, Ph.D., and Ruthellen Josselson, Ph.D., *Best Friends: The Pleasures and Perils of Girls' and Women's Friendships* (New York: Crown Publishers, Inc., 1998), p. 13.

## Chapter 2. Making Friends

1. Interview with Pat, age 14, November 16, 2000.
2. Interview with Marissa (real name withheld for privacy), age 17, January 31, 2001.
3. Interview with Katie, age 15, January 16, 2001.
4. Interview with Ryan, age 16, October 27, 2000.
5. Ellen Rosenberg, *Get a Clue—A Parent's Guide to Understanding and Communicating with Your Preteen* (New York: Henry Holt and Company, 1999), pp. 114–115.
6. Interview with Dr. Robin Beach, December 7, 2000.
7. Interview with Marissa.
8. Interview with Pat.
9. Interview with Dr. Beach.
10. David B. Pruitt, M.D., editor-in-chief, *Your Adolescent —The American Academy of Child and Adolescent Psychiatry* (New York: Harper Collins Publishers, Inc., 1999), pp. 36–37.
11. Ibid., p. 9.
12. Interview with Katie.
13. Interview with Jason, age 15, February 21, 2001.

## Chapter 3. The Three P's—Peer Pressure, Popularity, and Parents

1. Interview with Katie, age 15, January 16, 2001.

2. Laurence Steinberg, Ph.D., and Ann Levine, *You and Your Adolescent—A Parent's Guide for Ages 10–20* (New York: Harper Perennial, Revised edition, 1997), p. 190.

3. Interview with Tom, age 16, January 25, 2001.

4. Interview with Dr. Robin Beach, December 7, 2000.

5. Ellen Rosenberg, *Get a Clue—A Parent's Guide to Understanding and Communicating with Your Preteen* (New York: Henry Holt and Company, 1999), p. 175.

6. Allison Abner and Linda Villarosa, *Finding Our Way: The Teen Girls Survival Guide* (New York: Harper Collins, 1995), p. 226.

7. Interview with Jason, age 15, February 21, 2001.

8. Sharon Begley, "Special Report: A World of Their Own—They're Spiritual, Optimistic and Ambitious. How Teens Want to Shape the Future," *Newsweek*, May 8, 2000, p. 56.

9. Interview with Jill, age 14, February 22, 2001.

10. Steinberg, p. 185.

11. Interview with Tom.

12. Interview with Ryan, age 16, October 27, 2000.

13. Interview with Katie.

## Chapter 4. Dealing With Conflicts

1. Interview with Samantha, age 14, March 18, 2001.

2. Kate Cohen-Posey, *How to Handle Bullies, Teasers, and Other Meanies* (Highland City, Fl.: Rainbow Books, Inc., 1995).

3. Ellen Rosenberg, *Get a Clue—A Parent's Guide to Understanding and Communicating with Your Preteen* (New York: Henry Holt and Company, 1999), p. 122.

4. Ibid., p. 129.

5. Interview with Katie, age 15, January 16, 2001.

6. Rosenberg, pp. 130–131.

7. Interview with Marissa, (real name withheld for privacy), age 17, January 31, 2001.

8. Ibid.

## Chapter 5. Cliques

1. Interview with Jason, age 15, February 21, 2001.

2. Interview with Pat, age 14, November 16, 2000.

3. Interview with Katie, age 15, January 16, 2001.

4. David B. Pruitt, M.D., editor-in-chief, *Your Adolescent—The American Academy of Child and Adolescent Psychiatry* (New York: Harper Collins Publishers, Inc., 1999), p. 10.

5. Charlene C. Giannetti and Margaret Sagarese, *Cliques—8 Steps to Help Your Child Survive the Social Jungle* (New York: Random House, 2001), p. 20.

6. Interview with Jason.

7. Laurence Steinberg, Ph.D., and Ann Levine, *You and Your Adolescent—A Parent's Guide for Ages 10–20* (New York: Harper Perennial, Revised edition, 1997), p. 184.

8. Interview with Jason.

9. Interview with Samantha, age 14, March 18, 2001.

10. Giannetti and Sagarese, p. 30.

11. Ibid., pp. 30, 92, 101.

12. Interview with Jill, age 14, February 22, 2001.

## Chapter 6. How to Deal With Former Friends and Bullies

1. Interview with Marissa, (real name withheld for privacy), age 17, January 31, 2001.

2. Interview with Katie, age 15, January 16, 2001.

3. Interview with Pat, age 14, November 16, 2000.

4. Interview with Jill, age 14, February 22, 2001.

5. Ellen Rosenberg, *Get A Clue—A Parent's Guide to Understanding and Communicating with Your Preteen* (New York: Henry Holt and Company, 1999), p. 133.

6. Allison Abner and Linda Villarosa, *Finding Our Way: The Teen Girls' Survival Guide* (New York: Harper Collins, 1995), p. 233.

7. Interview with Samantha, age 14, March 18, 2001.

8. Charlene C. Giannetti and Margaret Sagarese, *Cliques—8 Steps to Help Your Child Survive the Social Jungle* (New York: Random House, 2001), p. 103.

## Chapter 7. High School Reunion—The Future Face of Teen Friendships

1. Interview with Jen, age 33, February 23, 2001.
2. Interview with Sue, age 29, February 15, 2001.
3. Interview with Lorrie, age 23, February 27, 2001.
4. Interview with Drew, age 26, February 22, 2001.
5. Interview with Mary, age 28, February 24, 2001.
6. Interview with Tom, age 22, February 22, 2001.
7. Interview with Lauren, age 33, February 16, 2001.
8. Interview with Lorrie.

# Further Reading

Abner, Allison and Linda Villarosa. *Finding Our Way: The Teen Girls' Survival Guide*. New York: HarperPerennial, 1995.

Carlson, Richard, Ph.D. *Don't Sweat the Small Stuff for Teens—Simple Ways to Keep Your Cool in Stressful Times*. New York: Hyperion, 2000.

Covey, Scan. *The 7 Habits of Highly Effective Teens*. New York: Fireside, 1998.

Daldry, Jeremy. *The Teenage Guy's Survival Guide*. Boston: Little Brown and Company, 1999.

Drill, Esther, Heather McDonald and Rebecca Odes. *Deal With It—A Whole New Approach to Your Body, Brain, and Life as a Girl*. New York: Pocket Books, a division of Simon & Schuster, Inc., 1999.

Pollack, William, Ph.D. *Real Boys: Rescuing Our Sons from the Myths of Boyhood*. New York: Random House, 1998.

# Internet Addresses

### Adolescence Directory On-Line (ADOL)
<http://www.education.indiana.edu/cas/adol/adol.html>
*Information on adolescent issues geared to parents, teachers, and teens. This Web site has a good collection of mental health and health resources with a section dedicated to resources exclusively for teens.*

### Teen City Central
<http://www.child.net/hscentral.htm>
*An online gathering place for high school students. The site includes games, chats, contests, teen journalism, as well as information on issues facing teens like dating, drugs, getting along with parents, prejudice and violence prevention.*

### TeenGrowth.com
<http://www.teengrowth.com>
*Created by a team of teens, doctors, and teachers who are committed to helping adolescents. Includes information on emotions, friends, cliques, school, and other relevant information for teens.*

# For More Information

**Alcohol and Drug Helpline**
1-800-821-4357

**National Latina Health Organization**
1-510-534-1362

**Suicide Prevention Hotline**
1-800-827-7571

**Youth Crisis Hotline**
1-800-448-4663

# Index